Memories in Focus

N.E. Ulster from
old photographs
1860 – 1960

Volume Four

Compiled & Edited
by Tom McDonald
& Robert Anderson

ISBN 0 948154 79 9

Printed and Published by
Impact Printing (of Coleraine) Ltd.
2 Stone Row, Coleraine, BT52 1EP, N. Ireland

This publication has received support from the
Cultural Traditions Group of the Community Relations Council.

Introduction

Ten years have passed since we published the first volume of *Memories in Focus*. The response to that and the subsequent Volumes II and III was amazing and very gratifying. Since 1986, when Volume III was published, we have been endeavouring to complete our selection for Volume IV by trying to fill any gaps which we felt existed, and we have yet again included many photographs which have never before been published.

Like Volume III we have used several photographs dating from the 1960s as there have been numerous changes since then. Our selection comes from a variety of sources including the collections held by various museums, but are mostly drawn from the collections of local individuals, to whom we are deeply grateful. Without such unselfish support a book of this quality and depth of interest would be impossible to produce and we have listed these friends in our acknowledgements section.

This volume represents the culmination of about 12 years' research and we feel that it should be the last- at least for the present. Over the years we have seen thousands of photographs in the process of selection for inclusion in the *Memories in Focus* Series and we feel that an interesting mix of views has been achieved which will help to record for posterity the changing nature of our surroundings, social history and traditions. The presentation and format of *Memories in Focus* has been widely copied throughout the Province. Few, though, have managed to achieve the high standards which we imposed on ourselves from the beginning nor contain as much historical detail and range of photographic sources.

We enjoyed compiling the Series and over the last 12 years have learned a lot about our area and the people who lived here. A great debt of gratitude goes to those photographers and collectors who made four volumes of *Memories in Focus* all possible.

Robert Anderson and Tom McDonald, 1992

To

Denise and Linda, Neal and Charlotte

Acknowledgements

Our thanks go to the following individuals and organisations for the loan of photographs and help with information for captions. Without their wholehearted co-operation the book would not have been possible.

Roy Anderson
Maxwell Blair
Robert W. Bacon
Laurence Crawford
Tommy Cecil
Hamill Family
Irwin Family
Hugh Kane
Willie Lake
Jim Leighton
Michael McMullan
Tommy Tinkler
Michael Thompson
Billy O'Neill
John McClements
Billy McCaughan
John Murray
McDonald Family
Coleraine Chronicle
Portstewart Golf Club
Ulster Museum
Library Headquarters, Ballymena

SURROUNDING AREAS

TRANSPORT

Coleraine

Pates' Lane

Plate 1

An unusual view over the town taken from the top of Pates' Lane in the late nineteenth century. The name Pates' Lane was derived from Peat's Row, called after the Peat Family. It also carried the name "Ragman's Row" in an old map. Major points of reference in the town are the large terraces of Millburn Road, the Customs House, Knox's houses at Hanover and St. Patrick's Church tower. On the Killowen side can be seen the Elim Church, founded by public appeal in 1869; Dunlop Street and the smoking stack of Gribbon's Flax Mill. The mill was the major employer in the town west of the Bann. This photograph was contained in a collection of Irish views published in America and which was recently returned to Coleraine.

Killowen Distillery

Plate 2

The distillery in Killowen has had a tenuous existence dating from the eighteenth century. It is recorded as being operated by McPeake and Hopkins in 1802 and to have ceased production in 1807. It was converted into warehouses but revived in 1917 by Brown, Corbett and Co. as the Killowen Distillery. In the 1930s Boyds of the Coleraine Distillery bought the Killowen complex to use for the malting of barley. It was reported at the time to be "a real shambles" and major renovations were required to make it suitable for this purpose . The chimney, carrying the name "Killowen" in glazed white brick, was a local landmark for many years

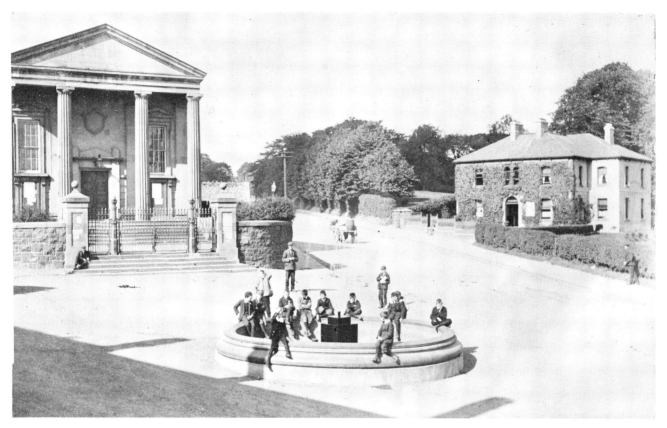

The Courthouse

Plate 3

Three features of Waterside make up this late 19th century scene. On the right stands the ivy-covered Cottage Hospital dating from 1891 which served the district as a hospital before Ratheane and which was itself then to become the Mary Ranken Maternity Hospital and Child Welfare Clinic. The fountain in the foreground was an ornamental feature, although judging from the group of young people, no water is evident on this day. The imposing Neo-Greek style building behind the fountain was built as the town's courthouse in 1852, the architect being Stewart Gordon, who was the county surveyor at the time. Unlike the other features in the photograph this building still stands although derelict and minus the splendid cast-iron gates. The courthouse ceased its function in July 1985.

Waterside Hotel

Plate 4

This pair of views illustrate shopfronts in Waterside and the former elegance of the Clothworker's Arms Commercial and Family Hotel. The business, also known as the Waterside Hotel, was built in 1844 at a cost of £2000 by John Lynn (who also built the bridge). It originally served travellers on the Coleraine - Londonderry railway. Until 1860 a station was situated at the rear of the hotel. The Waterside Station was connected with Coleraine Station by a coach service. The drapers shop occupying the corner opposite the hotel is Tannahills and Killowen Distillery chimney is visible in the background of the bottom scene. The photographs can almost be "dated" by the presence of the trees in Captain Street.

"Frederica"

Plate 5

One of the most striking photographs of Coleraine Harbour located in recent years is this one of the Canadian barquentine *Frederica*. The vessel had arrived at Coleraine from St. John's, New Brunswick, with a cargo of timber for the well-known local merchants H. & T. Bellas, on 9th June, 1899. Tom Bellas, a keen amateur photographer, many of whose negatives still survive, took this view of men unloading the ship through the special door in the vessel's bow. Ships such as *Frederica,* an impressive 543 tons, were a familiar sight in the port at the end of the 19th century and provided work for the tugs *Eagle* and *Confidence,* which were based at Coleraine. In fact, part of *Frederica's* cargo had to be off-loaded on to *Confidence* in Portstewart Bay so that she could come up the river to the port.(See Vol. II Plate 93).

Ferryquay Street   Plate 6

An aerial view showing the junction of Ferryquay Street and Hanover taken in the early 1960s. This area was always a focal point of the town featuring in history as far back as the 10th century when an Abbey existed close by. This abbey was raided by Vikings, who made their way up the Bann. The abbot was killed in the attack. Bones have been uncovered on occasions when digging has taken place in the area. Names of businesses in Hanover include Paddy McMains (fertilisers), Howden (potatoes), Stewart & Orr (produce), Murphy (furniture), McElderry (merchants), G.P.O. Garages, Morrow (vet) and Stuart (car showroom and garage). The area has been extensively redeveloped in recent years and none of the businesses now trade on these sites. (See Vol. III Plate 11).

Ramparts

Plate 7

A view of the rustic bridge in Anderson Park against a backcloth of The Ramparts and St. Patrick's Church. This is the only surviving section of the old fortified earth and stone wall which defended the Plantation town in the 17th century. Old Coleraine had been built within the Ramparts, which began at the junction of the Brook and the Bann, swung around the church following the line of Society Street and eventually turning west to meet the River Bann again. At that time gates in the Rampart were at King's Gate and Blind Gate, which gave these streets their names. Townspeople and refugees were using the church as a sanctuary when it was struck by a cannonball during an early conflict. No serious damage was recorded.

Circular Road Intersection

Plate 8

Until quite recently this triangle of buildings stood at the intersection of Circular Road and Brook Street at one of the busiest traffic routes in the town. On the left Brook Place, which once provided a slip road towards the town centre, is now the site of a modern housing development. At one time Brook Street was the main through route to Portrush and Portstewart and its Brook Place intersection carried traffic destined for Bushmills and Ballycastle. The steep hills at both ends of Brook Street led to the development of Millburn Road and Railway road as alternative routes to Portrush and Bushmills respectively. Two unusual trades listed for Brook Street in a 1910 directory were an aerated water manufacturer and a bill poster! (See Vol. III Plate 41).

Picture Palace

Plate 9

A photograph, full of interest, of Railway Road taken from what was then a car park. The foreground highlights a group of new Massey-Ferguson tractors and trailers, the first of their type to be introduced into the area, by Mr. Wilfred Mairs, proprietor of the Brook Garage, which can be seen on the right. Also prominent in the background is The Picture Palace or "Christies", which is fondly remembered by several generations of cinema-goers. The Irish Living Picture Co. had opened here in 1914. Previously films had been shown in the local Orange Hall. The familiar chug of the diesel generating plant operated by the cinema, and the long queues awaiting admission, were all part of the Railway Road scene. Completing the background is the stone-built facade of Smythe and McKee's Mill. This area is the site of the leisure centre and was formerly the Mill Dam. (See Vol. I Plate 1, Vol. II Plate 20).

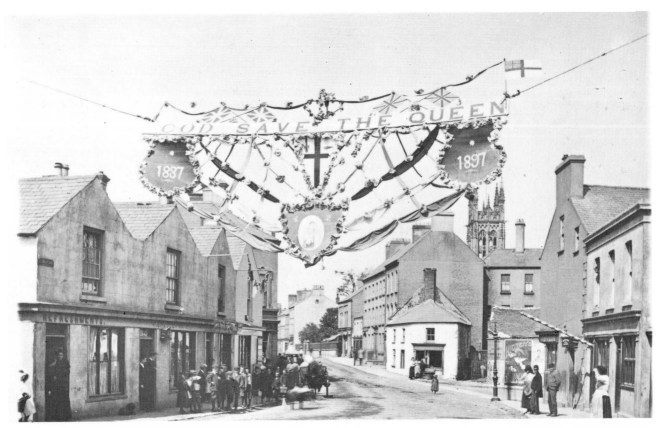

Alma Place

Plate 10

An historic event being commemorated with the erection of a garland celebrating the diamond jubilee of Queen Victoria in 1887. Left of the photograph shows Bradley's refreshment rooms and McNeill's grocery shop. In the centre is Johnston's fish shop at the junction of Brook Street, and on the right O'Kane's public house and McLeister's barbers, newsagents and tobacconist. One of the early Coleraine crests features in the centre of the garland. It was based on the arms of the City of London with the addition of a salmon, highlighting the London Company's involvement in the development of the borough and the importance of the salmon industry to the area. (See Vol. 1 Plate 9).

Masonic Hall

Plate 11

Erected in 1886, the Masonic Hall in Lodge Road was the meeting place of several local lodges. Lodge Road took its name from Hatton's Lodge to which the original Lodge Road, now Nursery Avenue, led. Early in the 1800s bricks for building many of the houses and shops in the town were manufactured at Lodge Farm at 20 shillings per 1000. Close by, in 1903, the first technical school was erected, opened in November, 1905. Gorteen House, owned by Moores the grocers of the Diamond, was next door. These two buildings now constitute the local R.U.C. Station. In 1861 Coleraine was headquarters of the R.I.C. in the county and district. They moved again to Abbey Street in 1866. Background left includes the square tower of the old St. Malachy's Chapel in Long Commons, and right, houses in the Long Commons and the rear of the Salvation Army Hall.

Long Commons

Plate 12

This street takes its name from the fact that most of the land at one time was common grazing ground. In 1734 the Irish Society noted that the corporation of Coleraine had enclosed some of it into gardens and this had led to complaints from the population. Gradually the Commons became confined to the area surrounding the former Irish Society School and the road leading to it retained the name Long Commons. The photograph shows the street's junction with Taylor's Row, named after the Taylor family of the Coleraine Distillery. Another street adjoining were Chapel Square (the local church having been granted a site to build in 1836), Boilingwell Lane and Dirty Lane. The barefoot lad and the bowler hatted gentlemen show a contrast in age and fortunes as do the single storey thatched dwelling and the much larger modern houses. (See Vol. III Plate 38).

Terrace Row Church

Plate 13

Third Coleraine Presbyterian Church was established in 1792 and the first building was situated in Waterside. The first minister was the Rev. James Hunter ordained four years later. The site of the present buildings was donated by the Irish Society in 1832 for an annual rent of £5. In the 1850s and early 1860s Presbytery Visitations recorded over 250 families with attendances exceeding 500 each Sabbath. An extension to the church seating was soon required. By 1891 the old church, which was "plain and out of date", was completely renovated and enlarged. Our photograph, which dates from the late 1940s, was taken before a meals kitchen to serve the Irish Society and other local schools, was built across the roadway between the schools and the local British Legion Clubrooms.

Ardbana House and Foundry

Plate 14

Ardbana House, the home of the Kennedy family, was erected on Mountsandel Road in 1879, adjacent to the three storey foundry building. The business commenced in this area in 1842 and grew to prosperity in Victorian times manufacturing threshing machines and other farm and industrial implements and machinery. Visible in the background is the 50 foot tower which contained the windmill used to drive a water pump. The Coleraine Distillery chimney can also be clearly identified. The advent of motorised agricultural equipment heralded the decline of the foundry. It survived in its later years manufacturing specialist spare parts for this motorised industry. The business eventually closed in 1953 and the site is now utilised as a car park. (See Vol. III Plate 29).

Baptist Church   Plate 15

The Baptist Church was established in Coleraine in 1795 initially occupying a corn store on the North Rampart at Bellhouse Lane. The present Church building at Abbey Street was opened on 29 March, 1842, when the generous collection at the opening services totalled £20. Rev. Freeman, one of the longest serving pastors of the congregation, was the first Coleraine minister to own a motor vehicle and was instrumental in establishing Churches in the surrounding area. The Jubilee Hall, serving as the Sunday School, was added in 1888/89 in the years following Queen Victoria's Jubilee.

The Diamond

Plate 16

Always the centre of activity, the Diamond, or Market Place as it was formerly known, takes on a more leisurely atmosphere in this early photograph. The Town Hall has its entrance door facing towards Bridge Street, railings surround the building and the ornamental urns on the clock tower are very much in evidence. Horse traffic is to the fore and horses are "parked" simply by placing a small bag of hay or oats on the ground in front of the animal. The streets were badly cut up and fouled by animals and "footpads" of cobblestones can just be seen across the road. The row of business premises on the right were the site of the last of the original Plantation houses with oaken frames. Their walls had been finished by studs nailed to frames and plastered with a clay mixed with hay and rushes.

Diamond Market   Plate 17

Taken about 1910 this photograph illustrates the Town Hall and the north side of the Diamond. In front of the recently-extended Town Hall the Crimean War cannon acts as a war memorial and as a focal point for a casual flax market. The buildings on the right, some of which had their origins in the early 1600's, house several of the area's best known businesses. These include the Northern Bank and Provincial Bank, Post Office, W. and J. Baxter, painter and decorator, Anderson, solicitors and Christies, general hardware merchants. The Diamond was the centre of banking activities and was the address also of the Belfast Bank and Ulster Bank all later to be joined by the Bank of Ireland and Coleraine Savings Bank. These served a 1910 town population of 7000 people. (See Vol. I Plate 31, Vol. III Plate 19).

Church Street Commerce

Plate 18

A photograph taken from the Lawrence Collection of Church Street and the Diamond around 1898. This was a leisurely age, no great bustle being apparent. On the left a couple amble arm-in-arm past Hill Brothers' drapery store. Behind them poultry hang outside Cameron's butchers shop, in the middle of the street a group of young boys, perhaps newspaper sellers, take an interest in the activities of the photographer, while nearby two men pass the time of day - one leaning on his bicycle. On the right is Boyds' seedmerchants with sacks of seeds and grain standing outside. Shopkeepers and their employees worked long hours in those times, perhaps 7.00 a.m. - 8.00 p.m. Only in 1905 was half-day closing introduced. The Town Hall seems very imposing with the lack of vehicular traffic and outside it is the Russian cannon, the war memorial of that time. (See Vol. I Plates 28. 29).

B.B. Silver Band

Plate 19

A scene at Church Street in the 1950s of the 2nd Coleraine Company Boys' Brigade Old Boys' Silver Band leading youth organisations. The Silver Band dates to 1922 having been preceded by a pipe band. Famous names associated over the years include Fred Watt, Johnny Leonard, Sandy Pearson and the Lake, Simpson, McDonald and McKay Families. The band is still to the fore in musical circles. Businesses in the street at this time include Bellas (hardware); Moore (draper); McKenna (public house); Cameron (butcher); Stevenson (haberdashery) and Goorwich (draper). Behind the crowd can be seen a sign advertising McCloskey's ladies' and gents' hairdressers. The photograph was taken from a second storey window of McAleese's grocery shop on the corner of Park Street.

Hero's Homecoming

Plate 20

Six months into the new century the town witnessed one of its most memorable events when Field Marshal Sir George White, VC, GCB, GCVO, GCI, GCIE, returned to his native town for a hero's welcome. (See Vol 1, Plate 40 and Vol II Plate 14). After a triumphant parade of the town Sir George was presented with a number of gifts including a silver cigar case and other mementoes. The procession shown in the photograph at Church Street was reported in great detail by the local press including graphic descriptions of the decorations in various streets of the town. Among the engagements carried out during the visit was the naming of Bann Rowing Club boats by Lady White. This was followed by races and an illuminated procession of boats on the river. The huge numbers accompanying and witnessing Sir George's carriage bore testimony to the esteem in which he was held by the local population.

Changing Shopfronts

Plate 21

A mid 1960s view of an almost deserted Church Street probably taken on a Sunday afternoon. This photograph is interesting in that practically all of the businesses shown have ceased to exist in the town. The only exceptions are the old established local firms of R. J. McCandless, who still occupy the same building as they have done since 1886, when John McCandless opened his ironmongery, plumbing and gasfitting business, and Simpson and Hill who are now situated in the Diamond having been established in 1934 in Queen Street, before moving to Church Street in 1939. Prior to the present troubles and the eventual pedestrianisation of the town centre, Church Street was a main arterial route with traffic passing through the heart of the town. It is hard to imagine that the hustle and bustle of a Saturday in Coleraine was, until recently, confined to the footpaths only!

Queen Street/Circular Road

Plate 22

Standing at the intersection of Queen Street, Circular Road and Millburn Road, the three-storey block of three houses which formed Castleview Terrace derived their name from the view which included the site of Drumtarsey Castle on the west bank of the Bann. The houses were built by Warren Baxter in 1855. In the background is the garage owned by the family of W.J. McCaughan, who also had premises in Portrush and Ballycastle. The building on the opposite corner of Circular Road was formerly a part of the premises of Christies Ltd, who manufactured fireplaces on the site. It later became a showroom for the Electricity Board. The terrace was demolished in the mid 1950's. Other large terraces which stood on Millburn Road included Clifton Terrace, Esdale Terrace and Fountain Villas. (See Plate 81).

Kingsgate Street Parade

Plate 23

A 'ladies only' element heads a parade making its way past St. Patrick's Church and into Kingsgate Street in the early part of the 1900s. The ladies and girls are wearing the large-brim hats and long outfits characteristic of the Edwardian era. Kingsgate Street derived its name from the fact that it was the site of one of the 'gates' allowing access to the walled town of troubled Plantation times. In the background can be seen the tobacconist and hairdressing premises of McDonald's and Edmiston's butchers shop. Various forms of transport make their way to and from Church Street and include jaunting cars, a working cart and a small donkey and cart. The reason for the parade is not known. (See Vol. II, Plate 14).

COLERAINE, CO. LONDONDERRY   R 5066

Aerial View   Plate 24

This magnificent aerial view of Coleraine and the River Bann was taken about 1955 and clearly illustrates just how much the town has expanded in the intervening years. Easily identified in the photograph are the harbour, with two steamers in port, the Gasworks, the Baptist Church, New Row, Killowen Distillery, the Manor House and Gribbon's Mill. Major developments which have since taken place in the area covered by the photograph are the building of the County Hall and the Health Centre, the re-development of the town centre, the demolition of Killowen Distillery and Gribbon's Mill and, more recently, the Gasworks. Also very noticeable is the lack of housing on Ballycairn Road.

Portstewart

'Hopley' Salvage   Plate 25

In Volume II of this series a photograph was used which dated from July, 1856, of the wreck of the American sailing ship *George A. Hopley* on Portstewart Strand. Since that volume was published this photograph of the encampment on the beach at the wreck has been discovered and it shows something of the activities at the site during the operation to salvage the valuable cargo from the ship. Many stories of the operation survive including the evergreen tale about the casks from the ship which were buried in the dunes and which, for years afterwards, provided tots of 'Hopley Rum' for the natives of Portstewart and Burnside. There is also a tale of "Bold McNeill" from old Portrush who was unfortunate enough to be the only person drowned in the salvage operations. (See Vol. II), Plate 34, Plate 36).

U.S. Army

Plate 26

Because of strict wartime censorship very few photographs exist of activities in and around the Triangle area during the Second World War. We were therefore very pleased to unearth this view of an anti-tank gun crew on Portstewart Strand in 1942. The soldiers are from the U.S. Army's 168th Infantry and were part of an anti-tank company whose billet was in Bright Cottage at the Hill in Portstewart. The 168th Infantry Headquarters were in White Hall Chambers in Coleraine and the soldiers were stationed all round the area including Downhill Castle, Cromore Estate and in the empty boarding houses in Portrush.

Dominican Convent, Portstewart. Reception Room.

Dominican Convent, Portstewart. A corner of the Library.

Dominican Interior   Plate 27

Two impressive views of the interior of the Dominican Convent in the 1920s, one the reception room and the other a corner of the library, which gives an indication of the elegance and comfort enjoyed by the landlord and successive owners of O'Hara's Castle. Twenty-one pupils, 16 of them boarders attended school here in September, 1917 a few months after six Dominican sisters had made "Rock Castle" their home. Many of the furnishings have been caringly retained and one of the larger tables is known to have been used by the landlord when tenants arrived or were summoned to pay their annual rents.

Class Distinction   Plate 28

A flag flutters over the castellated tower of the large house built in the promontory overlooking Portstewart by Henry O'Hara in 1834. Known as O'Hara's or Portstewart Castle, it features repeatedly in the many views available of the resort taken over the last century and a half. Less prominent, but just as significant in the history of the village, is the tiny thatched cottages known as Bone Row and occupied by the traditional fishing families. The tenants of one house pose in front of their home with a jaunting car. The irony of the class situation is that the cottiers would have been warmer in their snug thatched abodes that the occupants of the draughty castle. (See Vol. I, Plate 65.)

Slipway Crowd

Plate 29

Fishermen and locals gather on the slipway at the Harbour in the early 1890s as a catch is landed. Much has changed architecturally on this portion of the Promenade with the building of Henry's Carrig-na-Cule Hotel and grocery store, the Windsor Hotel and many larger houses. On the skyline Heathmount stands alone with the pinnacled battlement of the Methodist Church on the right. The Harbour itself consisted then of small basin ptotected by a single wall. There was no inner dock at this time. Boats in use were of the "dronthiem" sailing and pulling type and can be seen drawn up at the top of the slipway. Washing, possibly from one of the large houses, is being dried on the rocks in the centre of the photograph.

"Puffer"

Plate 30

The small Glasgow-registered steamer *Logan* unloading coal into a tiny lorry in Portstewart harbour about 1925. The *Logan,* at just over 66 feet long and 18 feet wide, was about the largest vessel which could enter the inner dock at Portstewart. She was owned by Dicksons of Glasgow and employed on the coastal coal trade. The coal being unloaded may have been for S. R. Henry, of the Carrig-na-Cule, who is known to have imported coal by this method. His use of the harbour in this way resulted in some criticism from the fishermen, who had to move their boats to accommodate the commercial traffic. This, despite Mr. Henry's generosity and patience towards the fishermen during the lean winter months when his business often extended credit to those who required it. (See Vol. I, Plates 49, 50; Vol. II Plate 50; Vol. III, Plates 48, 49, 87).

Henry's Corner

Plate 31

The popular "Henry's Corner" at the Carrig-na-Cule, which was once a feature of the world-famous North West 200 motorcycle road race, during an event in the early 1960s. S. R. Henry established the businesses on this corner site in the early 1900s. The race was first run in 1929 by The City of Derry and District Motor Club.

Famous riders who participated in the early years include Stanley Woods, Malcolm Templeton, Artie Bell, Geoff Duke and Jimmy Guthrie. Lap speeds read 59.41 m.p.h. in the 250cc class of 1929. Prize money in this year totalled £49 when a Rover car cost £250. (See Vol. I, Plate 60 and Vol. III, Plate 77).

Atlantic Circle

Plate 32

A curved terrace of 3-storey houses form Atlantic Circle, which is just off the Portmore Road. These houses were built about 1900. Clearly visible in the photo are the tracks of the Portstewart Tram, which ran from the south end of the resort's promenade to Cromore Station, on the outskirts of the town. Atlantic Circle was one of the tram's stopping points and people can be seen with their luggage awaiting the arrival of the tram to transport them to Cromore and their rail connections with the rest of the Province. Many of the large houses in Atlantic Circle were guest houses.

Portmore Garage

Plate 33

Standing just off Portmore Road between Atlantic Circle and the York Hotel was this little petrol station known as Portmore Garage and owned at the time of the photograph by W. Nicholson. The garage developed over the years and played an important role in the N.W. 200 motor cycle races when the pits were centred in this area. When Portmore Garage finally closed during the 1980's it had served the town for some 60 years as petrol station, garage, car salesroom and finally supermarket before being demolished and the site occupied by retirement flats and holiday homes.

Tram at Portmore

Plate 34

This rare view of the Portstewart tram was taken on Portmore Road. The tram is returning from Cromore towards the town and comprises the steam engine, a double-decked passenger car and a goods wagon. As mentioned earlier, the tram was established to provide a link between the town and the railway station at Cromore after landlord John Cromie refused to allow the railway access to Portstewart. Credited with being the first steam tram in Ireland, the operation lasted from 1882 until 1926. One of the steam trams is preserved at the Ulster Folk and Transport Museum. (See Vol. I, Plates 53, 54).

Railway Station

Plate 35

The railway station for Portstewart was situated at Cromore, some distance outside the town, due to the reluctance of local landlord John Cromie to allow the railway company access through his land to the town. He later regretted his decision and as a result helped to finance a tram, which connected the town with its railway station. This fine view of the station was taken in the 1950s, and shows the N.C.C. engine No. 71 standing at Cromore. The platform opposite the main station buildings was partially used to provide a halt at the University of Ulster when it opened at Coleraine in 1968. (See Vol. II, Plate 51).

Golf Club   Plate 36

The original Strand Course clubhouse which was built in 1909, a year after the opening of the links at the Strand Head, is seen here with some stalwarts of the club posed outside. They include from left (excluding car driver) Robert Moore, Fred Shelly, Hugh Eccles, John McFeeter, Robert Hunter, Bob O'Neill and Houston Todd. At this time a carriage operated eight times per day from Portstewart Promenade the fare being 3d (1.5p) return. Golf originated in the resort in 1894 at the "Old Course" on the Portrush Road when £16 was collected to start a club. Prices ranged from 1/– (5p) for daily membership to 7s 6d (37.5p) per month. Until 1939 ladies were accorded full membership. (See Vol. I Plate 56; Vol. III Plates 53, 57).

Portrush

Cloughorr House

Plate 37

Standing just off the main road from Portrush to Bushmills on the outskirts of Portrush is Cloughorr House which today is better known as Kellys. Named the Golf Links Hotel after the Golf Club was established just across the road, the building has had many additions and alterations since this photo was taken around 1910. Today the house and its additions are used as an entertainments complex comprising a restaurant, bars and several discos.

The Ladies' Clubhouse

Plate 38

The Ladies' Section of Royal Portrush Golf Club was in existence in 1892/93 after an extension of the Salisbury Terrace clubhouse provided some facilities for lady members. By 1899 the membership had grown to 290. The clubhouse in the photograph was opened in 1928 and shows a group of young exponents being tutored in the eary Thirties. Vehicles in the background include a Lancaster, an Austin Seven and a Morris Cowley Coupe. Famous lady members include Florence and May Hezlett, Rhona Adair, Zara Bolton, Maureen Madill and Claire Nesbitt.

Tram at Gasworks   Plate 39

A 3-car tram fronted by No. 20 which was one of the two new toast-rack type electric cars purchased for the inauguration of the overhead electric system in July, 1899, stands in front of the Tramway Depot in Causeway Street. In the background are the gasometers and other buildings of the Portrush Gasworks which commenced operations in 1867 and finally demolished in 1971. (See Vol. II Plate 74).

Simpson's Garage

Plate 40

Causway Street was the site of the garage and vehicle store belonging to H. Simpson and Co. in the late 1920s. The firm were agents for Ford cars and offered vehicles for hire. Outside the premises stood a hand-operated pump dispensing Pratts petrol and a locker full of Mobil oil. The cavernous interior of the "Belfast" roofed building was used extensively to garage vehicles belonging to summer visitors who had arrived in the resort for "the season". It was later occupied by McCaughans and for a short time by "Motorworld" car museum before being demolished in the late 1980's.

Golf Links

Plate 41

Royal Portrush Golf Club was founded in 1888 as the County Club. The links were sited in the 40-acre triangle owned by the Earl of Antrim beside the railway station and consisted of nine holes but no clubhouse. It was encouraged and supported by the railway company, who owned the Northern Counties Hotel, most golfers of that era being visitors. Those staying in the hotel played free of charge. The annual subscription then was one guinea. Another nine holes were added together with a hut near Salisbury Terrace. The clubhouse in the photograph was built and opened in 1892 at a cost of £1300 and was in direct telephone communication with the railway station and Northern Counties Hotel. It lasted as home to the Men's Club until 1946 when it became the local British Legion Clubrooms. (See Vol. II Plates 75, 76, 77, 78; Vol. III Plate 60).

Ladies' Bathing Place

Plate 42

Perhaps one of the earliest views which we have published of "The Arcadia" or "Ladies' Bathing Place" shows yet another large gathering of people to what may have been a religious meeting. The arcadia is seen as a simple shack before any of the many improvements and extensions had taken place. Open air religious meetings were a common feature of the summer season at popular seaside resorts and this bathing place, allocated for ladies and children in this puritanical Victorian period, formed a natural amphitheatre. (See Vol. I, Plates 96, 97; Vol. II, Plates 72, 73; Vol. III, Plate 74).

Station Square

Plate 43

The unmistakable outline of *HMS Hood* forms the impressive background of this view of the Station Cafe, Station Square and the Harbour. Built in 1918 the *Hood* was just one of the many warship visitors to Portrush during the period between the wars. She was lost in action against the *Bismarck* in 1941. In the foreground period vehicles have come to park in front of the entrance to the station cafe (Vol I Plates 81, 82, Vol III Plate 63) which was attached to the magnificient station building of 1892. It is likely that most of these cars are in fact taxis awaiting the arrival of trains from Belfast and Londonderry.

Bus Depot

Plate 44

A 1950s view of the bus station in the resort. Most people who travelled to Portrush by bus will remember the area like this with the practical bus shelters. The regular services to Portstewart and Coleraine departed from the right hand side of the main shelter while excursion and special buses were to be found on the open area to the left of the picture. The main entrance to Barry's Amusements is also situated here and during the holiday season many thousands passed through these gates daily to thrill on the dodgems, the ghost train and the big wheel.

Pleasureground   Plate 45

The poster on the pillar in the foreground gives a clue to the event taking place on the area known variously as "The Pavilion" or the "Pleasuregrounds", beside the Station Square. The poster advertises a special evangelical mission to be held in Portrush on Sunday, 1st June and to be addressed by Mr. G. Govan. Among the assembled crowd are ladies and gents in classical Edwardian dress and a group of Boys' Brigade complete with pill box hats and haversacks. Beyond the crowd are a bandstand and the Golf Hotel. In front of the stone wall stands a typical horse trough of this period.

The Pavilion, Portrush

Skating Rink and Station Cafe

Plate 46

Entitled 'The Pavilion' in this postcard view is one of the focal points for tourists to Edwardian Portrush. On the left is the rear of the Station Dining Rooms featuring the windows and balcony offering superb sea views. The pagoda-style bandstand frequently hosted open-air concerts, pierrot shows and religious gatherings. The Skating Rink was a very popular venue for roller skaters and the whole site was the forerunner of the now famous Barry's Amusements. (See Vol. III, Plate 63).

Warship Plate 47

In the past many famous warships have paid courtesy visits to the resort of Portrush and names such as *Hood*, *Rodney* and *Drake* are well remembered in the town. But what of *HMS Wiston?* This small minesweeper called into the harbour on Friday 6th March, 1964, to land the Flag Officer for Northern Ireland and Scotland, Vice-Admiral Sir Arthur Hezlet, a native of the area. Seldom have warships actually entered Portrush Harbour and on this occasion the task was made even more difficult by the presence of the then regular container vessel *Wirral Coast* and the coaster *Silverthorn* loading stones at the "bins" M1205 *H.M.S. Wiston*, a 'ton' class minesweeper of 425 tons and under the command of Captain McCloud, RN, left the port after a brief stay moored alongside *Wirral Coast*.

Harbour Gaslight

Plate 48

A photograph of the harbour area, which at first glance seems empty, contains many interesting activities and features. Gas lighting and the branch railway line serving the quayside were both established in 1866. Next to the gas lamp sits a boarding gangway utilised by the Portrush/Glasgow steamers. Berthed alongside is a sailing ship unloading on to a horse and cart with a goods waggon standing behind. In the centre a pile of material, probably iron ore, awaits export. The buildings in the background form the oldest part of the town, which developed around the old dock before the present harbour was built in 1827.

Harbour Scene   Plate 49

Still fresh in a lot of people's memories are the fishing boats, pleasure cruisers and air-sea rescue launches in Portrush Harbour. Our photograph was, in fact, taken over 20 years ago and shows local boatman Jimmy Stewart setting out on an angling trip from the harbour in his boat *Girl Phyllis*. In the background are from left the Dohertys' *Queen Elizabeth,* used for almost 25 years to operate trips around the Skerries for 2s 6d (12.5p); the fishing boats *Scott; Cutty Sark, Fair Isle,* and *Family Friend* and the RAF air/sea rescue launch 2757 which was one of several based at the resort from 1963-1971. All these craft have disappeared from the local scene but 2757 remains as an exhibit at the RAF Museum in Hendon, the sole survivor of her class.

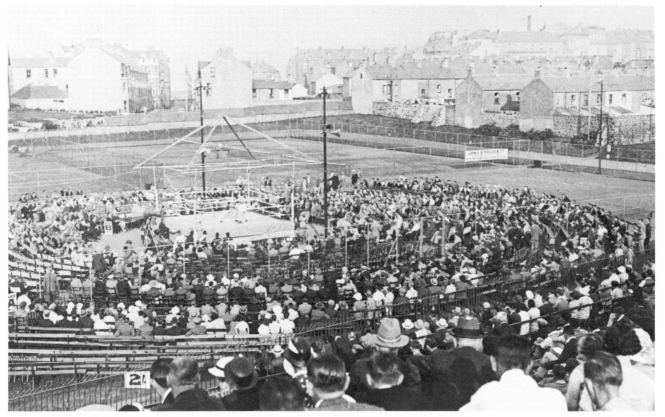

Boxing Tournament

Plate 50

This unusual scene took place at the Recreation Grounds on Tuesday, 10th July, 1934, during an International Police Boxing Tournament organised by the R.U.C. Athletics Association, under the guiding influence of Captain T. D. Morrison, later to become City Commissioner. The bout featured is a Germany v. Ireland contest and the Swastika was displayed by the German team. The 2s (10p) seats offered a distant view of the ring. The background includes Princess Street and the area of Ramore Street which was later re-developed. The chimney on the skyline belonged to the Northern Counties Hotel.

Fawcett's Hotel

Plate 51

A view in the 1950s of Fawcett's Royal Portrush Hotel standing at the corner of Mark Street and Main Street. Although not evident from the photograph this period was one of the busiest for hoteliers in the area in recent times. This was due in no small measure to the enterprise of people like the Fawcett family who were forerunners in organising "package" holiday by bus taking in many of the Province's tourist attractions. On the opposite side of the street stands the Olympia Cafe and to the left of the photograph can be seen part of the Northern Counties Hotel. (See Vol III Plate 68).

Antrim Arms Hotel   Plate 52

This photograph, one of the earliest in existence of the Antrim Arms Hotel caused great excitement and interest when it was loaned for inclusion. Opened in 1837 the hotel was the first in the resort serving mainly visitors to the world famous Giant's Causeway. By 1855 the railway had arrived in the town and in 1891 the Antrim Arms was purchased by the railway company and renamed the Northern Counties Hotel. The disastrous fire in March, 1990, totally destroyed the well-known landmark, including the ballroom dating from July, 1905, and the sea-water indoor swimming pool of 1935. Also lost was the imposing staircase and the grand wood panelling of the resident's lounge. (See Vol. I Plate 94; Vol II Plate 65, 67; Vol. III Plate 69).

White House Staff

Plate 53

Staff of the famous White House in Main Street pose outside their workplace along with two postmen and their wicker handcarts. At this time, in addition to the well-known Irish Linen trade, the White House carried on a world-wide exclusive tailoring business with clientele wooed by extensive advertising throughout the Empire. Orders were dispatched daily to destinations such as Hong Kong, Singapore, India and even to the Czar of Russia. The largest order to be exported was to a wholesale firm in Brisbane, Australia. As a result of this volume of mail order business, Portrush had a proportionately large Post Office in Causeway Street. Although this mail order business has ceased the White House has expanded considerably and today remains one of the premier stores in the area. (See Vol. I Plate 93; Vol. II Plates 68, 69).

Main Street Looking North

Plate 54

The Londonderry Arms Hotel, the Trocadero Cafe and the White House Store form the central portion of this view of Main Street in the late 1890s. The combination of Edwardian fashion, gas street lighting and the air of peace and tranquility portray a relaxed summer scene.

An Irish art exhibition is being held in the church hall of Holy Trinity parish. This hall was formerly a schoolhouse. To the left is Chalmers, family grocery and confectionery shop. Mr. Chalmers was prominent in local council affairs at this time.

Main Street, Portrush

92602

Middle Main Street   **Plate 55**

Another Main Street photograph, taken further along and at a later date also holds much of interest. The eye is immediately drawn to the two forms of transport, one the traditional horse and cart, the other the then innovative combination of motorcycle and sidecar. Cafes also feature prominently with the Cecil Cafe, with its distinctive curved windows dating from 1911, Blacks and another establishment offering dinners and teas. The building with the round tower was the Belfast Bank, now the Northern Bank built 1898. The style of dress dates the scene to the early 1920s.

Flooding at Dhu Varren   **Plate 56**

The Dhu Varren area, including Coleraine Road, Portstewart Road and Brooklyn Terrace, suffered serious flooding over the period 24/25 August, 1960, when 4.82 inches of rain fell during a 24-hour period. Culverts carrying two small streams became blocked resulting in the need for fishermens' punts and tractors to rescue people and belongings from homes. It was estimated that the water reached a depth of six feet in places in the Dhu Varren area, while on Coleraine Road it was recorded at three feet deep. The photograph was taken from a vantage point on the Portrush/Coleraine railway embankment.

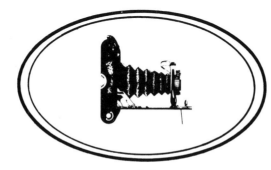

Surrounding Areas

Articlave

Plate 57

Articlave, which means "the height of the house of swords", is the oldest settlement in the Parish of Dunboe. It was the original London Clothworkers' village and by 1622 consisted of a huddle of cottages. The earliest settlers were lowland Scots, who arrived during the Plantation period. Prior to the 17th century the area round the village was an important farming distinct with the Sconce Hill Fort dominating. Our photogragh dates from the early 1900s and highlights the thatched single storey dwellings which made up most of this quiet backwater.

Castlerock Seafront

Plate 58

Sir Hervey Bruce's insistence on a railway station at the seaside village of Castlerock to serve Downhill Castle played a major part in the development of the resort. By November, 1860, through trains were running between Belfast and Londonderry and each one was required to stop at Castlerock. A development of this was that "Villa Tickets" were issued to owners of larger houses enabling them to commute to the cities. The first of these houses were Cliff House, Love's Hotel, Maritima, Miramar and Rock Ryan. The Bruce connection with the resort, which determined that any development should be to their liking, ended after the Second World War. Prior to this Castlerock had remained a rather exclusive residential area. The photograph is of a number of seafront bungalows which are now fronted by an extensive sea wall and promenade.

Downhill

Plate 59

This view of Downhill taken during the 1950s shows clearly the Downhill Hotel and railway station. The line, which ran from Londonderry to Coleraine, required extensive tunnelling through the basalt cliffs in this area. On the right of the photograph the track enters a tunnel which was ceremonially started by Lady Bruce igniting a charge of powder in 1845. The following year during more blasting operations the Railway Company's steamer *The Admiral* was anchored offshore with an invited party of guests to witness the dislodging of 16,000 tons of cliff face. In the background is the long curve of Downhill, Benone and Magilligan beaches which hosted motor-cycle racing, gliding and other sports activities over the years.

Ballyrashane Creamery

Plate 60

Ballyrashane Co-Op Society was formed in 1896 following a period of discussion which had lasted for 3 years. Farmers were concerned about the price they were getting for their butter from the Coleraine Butter Company and other similar operations. It was finally agreed to build a Creamery at Ballyrashane and farmers were asked to subscribe £1 for every cow they owned in order to finance the Society. Ballyrashane thus became the third Co-Operative Creamery in Ireland being registered in Dublin with the registration number 3. In the early days milk was brought into the Creamery, separated into cream and skimmed milk with the milk being returned to the farmer. In 1900 less than half a million gallons were received compared to over 20 million gallons today. Of course today many more diverse products are available with butter being exported as far afield as Saudi Arabia.

Portballintrae   Plate 61

The small seaside village of Portballintrae, as photographed by Valentines around 1900, was a popular place even in the mid 1760s when one of its fine houses was advertised is the Belfast Newsletter as "Lodgings for bathers or those with a mind to drink the salt water". The village was also known as Seaport and this connotation still survives in the name of a house, 'Seaport Lodge', built by the Leslies of Leslie Hill, Ballymoney in 1780. The village also has the unenviable reputation of being the only place in Ireland on which German shells fell in World War One. A passing steam coaster, the *Wheatear* was fired on by a German U-boat off Runkerry. All of the protectiles missed their intended target but some fell in and around the village causing some damage and not a little panic.

Royal Hotel, Giant's Causeway

Plate 62

The Giant's Causeway once boasted two large hotels - Traill's Causeway Hotel and Kane's Royal Hotel. The Royal was developed from a small white washed farmhouse in the 1860s by Mrs Francis Kane, formerly Miss Campbell, owner of the Antrim Arms Hotel, Bushmills. It was granted royal patronage when the Duke of Connaught visited the area. There was open rivalry between the two establishments because of Traill's involvement in the tramway operation. Porters from the Royal were not allowed to enter the nearby terminal building. The Royal was renovated and enlarged in 1890 and, ironically, by 1910 Kane owned both hotels. During the 1960s The Royal Hotel was demolished and the site is now occupied by Moyle Council's Visitors' Centre.

Upper Main Street, Bushmills

Plate 63

The town of Bushmills takes it name from the fact that it grew up around the flour, paper and spade mills which existed close by a bridge over the River Bush. However, the most important and well-known industry in the town is that of whiskey making. The Distillery was granted a licence in 1608 making it the world's oldest distillery and this street leads to its entrance. The houses on both sides were demolished in recent times, those on the right being replaced by modern dwellings and the other side becoming a car park. The Main Street Presbyterian Church and Hamill Hall are seen in the background.

McCambridge's Shop, Ballycastle

Plate 64

A well-known business of latter years situated at the corner of Market Street and the Diamond, Ballycastle, was the general store of E. F. McCambridge. Newspapers, tobacco, hardware and even prams could be purchased here. The hoarding covering an alleyway on the right is used to advertise the nearby cinema in Market Street. Admission prices vary from 1s 3d (8p) for the back stalls, to 6d (2.5p) for a seat in the pit. The Irish News features "Battle rages between Americans and Japanese" while films to be seen were "Private Lives" with Norma Shearer and Sylvia Simms in "You only live once". The period was the early 1940's.

Rathlin Island Jetty

Plate 65

The export of limestone from Rathlin Island provided work for some of the islanders as well as others from the mainland. This photo shows a small steamer alongside the jetty at Killeaney in Church Bay about to load quarried limestone from waggons. The limestone was quarried from the cliffs nearby and was exported to the Clyde where it was used in the steel making process.

Limestone was also exported from nearby Larrybane Quarry and from Glenarm both on the mainland. Islanders working at the quarry often set out before dawn to walk to their jobs and didn't return until after dark. Quarrying operations lasted only a few years. The photo dates from around 1910.

Balnamore Mill

Plate 66

Since the 18th century the Ballymoney district had a tradition of growing and beetling flax and weaving linen as a cottage industry. In 1805 a survey of 401 houses on the Leslie Hill Estate located 220 weavers. In 1876 the mill at Balnamore employed 420 spindles which grew to 12,000 by 1957, two years before its closure, which was brought about by a decline in the linen trade and the death of the owner Dr William McCleery. The 5-storey, 65,000 sq ft. building had a water wheel to drive its machinery. In the 1910's work started at 6 am for 6 days a week for a wage of 9/– (45p). During the second World War employment was at its peak with 400 on one shift.

Transport

Coleraine Coachbuilders

Plate 67

This photograph was taken outside Hamill's coachbuilding works in Limemarket Street around 1905 and shows some of the skilled tradesmen with an example of their craft. The Reid's Bakery bread waggon was just one of the many fine hand-crafted carts and vehicles for which Hamills were renowned. Started by Archibald Hamill in 1895, the firm developed from small beginnings. It is known that many local firms regularly had vehicles built here including Reid's Bakery, H. & T. Bellas, Ballyrashane Creamery and McDonald's, who bought horse-drawn carts. The firm is also believed to have built the first mobile library in the early 1950s, and were forerunners in the spraying of cellulose paint by the mid-1950s, having a purpose-built spray booth incorporated in the newly-constructed paint shop in Mountsandel Road. (See Vol. III, Plate 2.

McArthur's Visit

Plate 68

An historic event captured in Ballymoney of Kennedy Kane McArthur (seen in the front passenger seat of the Rozengarde car) on his triumphant return to his native district after winning a gold medal in the 1912 Olympics in Stockholm. McArthur, a native of Dervock, emigrated to South Africa to join the police at the age of 24. Always a keen distance runner, he was eventually chosen to represent his adopted country in the marathon event in the Swedish Olympics. He won the gruelling race out of a field of 68 runners and turned down lucrative offers in America to return home for a visit. He received a hero's welcome with banners, fireworks and masses of jubilant admirers greeting him at Ballymoney Railway Station. He returned to South Africa in 1913 and died there in 1960.

Unloading at Portrush

Plate 69

A scene of activity on the quayside at Portrush about 100 years ago as a small cart is filled with large sacks from the hold of a coastal sailing vessel. The ship is probably a ketch and her bowsprit can be seen to the left of the horse. The cart is of a type very common before the advent of motor transport. Unloading and loading by hand was a slow labour-intensive task with the dockers having to walk a plank or gangway from the ship to shore either carrying boxes, bags or bales or pushing wheelbarrows if the cargo was in bulk.

Coleraine Bus Mishap

Plate 70

A bus belonging to H.M.S. Catherwood is seen here with its nose in a garden of Bannview Villas on the Millburn Road. Although the cause of the accident isn't known the event seems to have caused considerable interest as quite a few cyclists have gathered to inspect the damage. The Catherwood firm took over many of the small local bus operations run by people such as Curtis Galt and John McDonald of Coleraine, Peter Doherty of Portstewart and Wallace Kennedy of Portrush. Catherwoods itself was eventually taken over by the U.T.A. The Ordnance Survey Memoirs of 1835 reported 32 horsedrawn cars constantly employed from Coleraine to Portstewart and Portrush and back again making two journeys each day.

O'Neill's Ices

Plate 71

In these days of multi-choice varieties of ice-cream and cavalcades of "chiming" sales vans many of the older generation will fondly remember an ice-cream 'slider' or 'poke' as an occasional treat when the only flavour available was vanilla. These were sold from a variety of simple outlets, one of the more unusual being the tricycle shown in the photograph. Edward O'Neill, who had been given a family recipe by an Italian friend established a business in Meeting House Street and later Roddenfoot. The daily routes of vehicles such as this included Ballymoney and Coleraine, as well as Dervock, Cloughmills and Balnamore and were serviced by sons who joined the family business.

Busy Port

Plate 72

This striking view of a very busy Coleraine Harbour was taken in 1960, just a few years before steamers were to disappear from the scene. Included in the photo are the motor vessel *Silverthorn* and the steamers *Bannspur* and *Banntrade*r with another unidentified motor vessel forward of *Silverthorn*. Coal is being discharged from *Silverthorn* and at least one of the steamers also has a coal cargo, while on the quayside stand piles of round timber awaiting export to South Wales for use as pit props in the mines there. The last steam ship to visit Coleraine was in 1963. The steamers carried only around 400 tons and were being replaced with motor ships carrying about 900 tons. Vessels using Coleraine port today can carry up to 2000 tons. (See Vol. I Plates 33, 34; Vol. II Plates 13, 95; Vol. III Plate 7).

Signal Cable Laying   Plate 73

The southern end of the platform at Coleraine railway station provides the backdrop for this unusual view of men engaged in laying cables for an improved signalling system in August, 1938. On the right can be seen the *Glenarm Castle*, a steam locomotive operating on the Derry Central line. The photograph was taken by A.R. Hogg, a well known Belfast-based commercial and industrial photographer. In this period the railway system extended to a total of 271 miles and in 1938 the railway carried almost 3 million passengers and 500,000 tons of freight.

Bank Building, Coleraine Diamond

Plate 74

Once a familiar sight and now almost non-existent the horse and cart were, until the advent of motor transport, indispensable in hauling a variety of goods around the streets. The cart seen here is loaded with building bricks for the new Bank of Ireland under construction in the Diamond in 1922. Milk, bread, coal and grocery deliveries were all undertaken by horse-drawn vehicles at this time. An interesting feature of the building work is the wheelbarrow full of bricks being hoisted aloft by a simple sheerlegs crane. Next door to the rising bank is Edgar's tearooms which became the newsagents and tobacconists of Evan Cox in later years. (See Vol. II Plate 5).

Tram, Train and Truck   Plate 75

The Station Square at Portrush provides the location for a variety of the modes of transport available to travellers arriving at the Victorian railway station. Alighting passengers could avail of the famous Giant's Causeway tram to extend their journey to Bushmills, Portballintrae or the Causeway itself. Hotels and major guest houses made use of waggons and jaunting cars to convey their clients and their luggage while horse and cart serviced the commercial and business communities with goods deliveries.

Horse Ploughing

Plate 76

A common rural sight up until the early 1950s was the ploughman and his team working in the fields. This photograph is of James Leighton of Bellemont, Coleraine, ploughing with Clydesdales *Kate* and *Jane* while the owner, Jimmy Young walks alongside. They were competing in a horse ploughing competition where prizes would have been awarded for workmanship and turnout. The harness and brasses had hours of labour spent on them and everyone rose early on competition day to plait manes and tails, rub down the animals and wash the "feathers" on their legs. There were, as now, horse ploughing societies and a good man was held in high repute as was a balanced working team which was judged on size, colour and compatibility.

Hugh T. Barrie Garage

Plate 77

Hugh T Barrie was a prominent Coleraine figure in late Victorian times. In 1880 he was advertising for ryegrass, hay and straw with premises in Rosemary Lane (Park Street) and Waterside (the old Railway Station). He lived in the Manor House and was a town commissioner, MP for North Derry and the first person in Coleraine to sign the Ulster Covenant. He gave the site in Union Street on which the Orange Hall was built. This photograph shows some of his vehicles garaged at Waterside. From left they are a Foden steam waggon, an Essex motor car, an Albion lorry, a Leyland lorry and a stone crusher.

Millburn Road Railway Bridge

Plate 78

A photograph taken within most readers' memory of a bridge which spanned the Millburn Road for over 100 years. It had served the main Coleraine - Londonderry line when this route used the original wooden Bann railway bridge (1860 - 1924) as well as the Harbour Railway from 1892 by way of a junction situated on the river side. The replacement bridge for the re-aligned rail route over the present river crossing is just visible in the background. The Harbour branch line was eventually closed in 1963 and the bridge and embankment were removed and the area landscaped a few years later. This photograph is dated 1966.

Jubilee Bridge

Plate 79

The tram connection between Portrush and Bushmills, which had been established in 1883, was extended to the Giants Causeway in 1887. This required a bridge across the River Bush near Portballintrae, and was achieved with a 3-span lattice girder bridge built by Maclellan of Glasgow. The structure incorporated two massive masony piers which carried the 133ft span 25ft above the river level. The bridge was named the "Victoria Jubilee Bridge" in recognition of the fact that it was constructed in the year of Queen Victoria's Jubilee. The bridge stood for almost 90 years and was demolished in the 1970s.

KERR STREET AND HARBOUR, PORTRUSH.

Harbour Branch Line

Plate 80

The quayside at Portrush Harbour was at one time served by a branch line from the railway station in Eglinton Street. As can be seen from the photograph, the line swept from the station to follow the line of Kerr Street, passed over a bridge at the 'wee dock' and on to the Harbour. The branch line was just under a mile in length and had been built in 1866 at a cost of £2950 and for a time steam engines were not permitted on this section of track and horses had to be used to move the waggons. No passengers were conveyed. Mixed gauge track was laid in 1883 to accommodate goods traffic from the Causeway Tramway, consisting of iron ore and limestone trains. Our photograph shows an excursion train shunted onto the track in the 1930s to leave space at the platforms at the station.

McCaughan's Garage, Ballycastle

Plate 81

The premises of one of the oldest families in the motor trade is featured in this photograph taken at Market Street, Ballycastle, in the early 1920s. The McCaughans, who lived above this bicycle and motorcycle shop, went on to run very successful businesses in Ballycastle, Coleraine and Portrush. In the photograph are two interesting motorcycles, one with a bathtub sidecar. The policeman, on the left of the doorway, would have been stationed in the building next door. A ledger from the Ballycastle business notes a gallon of Shell petrol at 2s 2d (11p). This was dispensed in 2 gallon cans for which a deposit of 3s (15p) was charged. Carbide lamps could be recharged or 4lbs of carbide bought for 1s 6d (75p). An advertisement of the era offered a Raleigh bike at £4.19s 6d with terms available.

Roadworks

Plate 82

This press photograph of a roadworks scheme in Captain Street, Coleraine, was taken in 1955 when local quarry owners R. J. Maxwell and Son were involved in a major road improvement scheme within the town. The vehicles in the photograph are mostly Bedford lorries which were favoured by the firm when they had a fleet of around 20. One interesting aspect of the job in Captain Street was that the pump, which provides a constant source of pure spring water, would be retained. The family firm of R. J. Maxwell and Son was established at Bushtown just outside Coleraine at the turn of the century. The move to Coleraine took place on 1936 but the family connection ended in 1953 with the death of Howard Maxwell. The firm was taken over by William Bolton in 1954 but continued to use the Maxwell name as was the case when it was again taken over, this time by the Thompson group, in 1971.

Bibliography

Books

Anderson R. and McDonald T. – *Memories in Focus Vol I* .... Ballycastle 1981

Anderson R. and McDonald T. – *Memories in Focus Vol II* .... Ballycastle 1983

Anderson R. and McDonald T. – *Memories in Focus Vol III* .... Ballycastle 1986

Anderson R. and Wilson I – *Ships and Quaysides of Ulster* .... Belfast 1990

Anderson R. --*The Port of Coleraine* .... Ballycastle 1976

Archibald W. – *The Development of Portstewart* .... M.A. Thesis 1977

Arnold J. – *The N.C.C. Saga* .... Devon 1973

Bamford J. L. – *Royal Portrush G C - A History* .... Ballycastle 1988

Boyd H. A. – *Ballycastle Narrow Gauge Railway* .... Notes

Currie J. R. L. – *The Northern Counties Railway Vols, I and II* .... London 1973/74

Currie J. R. L. – *The Portstewart Tramway* .... Lingfield 1968

Dallat C. – *A Tour of the Causeway Coast* .... Belfast 1988

Girvan W. D. – *U. A. H. S. Coleraine and Portstewart* .... Belfast 1973

Girvan W. D. --*U. A. H. S. North Antrim* .... Belfast 1972

Mullin F. E. – *The Causeway Coast* .... Belfast 1974

Mullin T. H. – *Coleraine in Modern Times* .... Belfast 1979

McCreary A. – *Spirit of the Age* .... Belfast 1983

McGuigan F. – *The Causeway Tram* .... Belfast 1983

Patterson E. M. – *The Ballycastle Railway* .... Devon 1965

Wilson I. – *Shipwrecks of the Ulster Coast* .... Ballycastle 1979

Periodicals

Coleraine Chronicle

Northern Constitution

Derry and Antrim Year Books

Others

O. S. Memoirs

Town Guides